# Environments and Energy

HOUGHTON MIFFLIN

BOSTON

Printed in the U.S.A.    ISBN-13: 978-0-547-06232-7    ISBN-10: 0-547-06232-X    2 3 4 5 6 7 8 9-0868-16 15 14 13 12 11 10 09

# Do What Scientists Do

Meet Fernando Caldeiro, the astronaut. His friends call him Frank. He is training to go into space. When he is not training, he tests computer programs used to run the space shuttle. Before Mr. Caldeiro became an astronaut, he tested new jets. He also worked on space shuttle rockets.

Frank Caldeiro is floating in a jet that gives the feeling of low gravity. This jet is one tool scientists use to learn more about space.
The jet's nickname is the "vomit comet." Can you guess why?

# Many Kinds of Investigations

Astronauts carry out many investigations in space. Sometimes they observe Earth and take photos. Other times they do experiments. They may test how plants or animals react to low gravity. They share what they find out with other scientists.

Astronauts learn to fly the space shuttle in machines called simulators. They also learn to use space shuttle tools to collect information.

# You Can...

# Think Like a Scientist

Everyone can do science.
To think like a scientist you have to:

▶ ask a lot of questions.

▶ find answers by investigating.

▶ work on a team.

▶ compare your ideas
to those of others.

**What is this lizard
doing? Is it sleeping?
Is it waiting for insects
to fly by? Or, is it doing
something else?**

# Use Critical Thinking

When you know the difference between what you observe and what you think about your observation, you are a critical thinker. A fact is an observation that can be checked to make sure it is true. An opinion is what you think about the facts. When you ask someone, "How do you know that?" you are asking for facts.

The lizard lies under the heat lamp for a while. Then it gets food. **I wonder if it must warm up before it can move around?**

I read that a lizard's body temperature falls when the air cools. It warms itself by lying in the sun.

# Science Inquiry

You can use **scientific inquiry** to find answers to your questions about the world around you. Say you have seen crickets in the yard.

**Observe** It seems like crickets chirp very fast on some nights, but slowly on other nights.

**Ask a question** I wonder, does the speed of cricket chirping change with temperature?

**Form an idea** I think crickets chirp faster when it's warmer.

**Experiment** I will need a timer and a thermometer. I will count how many times a cricket chirps in 2 minutes. I will do this when the air temperature is warmer and when the air temperature is cooler.

**Conclusion** I counted more chirps in warmer air temperatures. This result supports my idea. Crickets chirp faster when it is warmer.

Scientific inquiry includes communicating what you learn. You can tell about your experiment in words or drawings. Tell others to try it themselves. You can expect them to get the same results.

# Inquiry Process

Here is a process that some scientists follow to answer questions and make new discoveries.

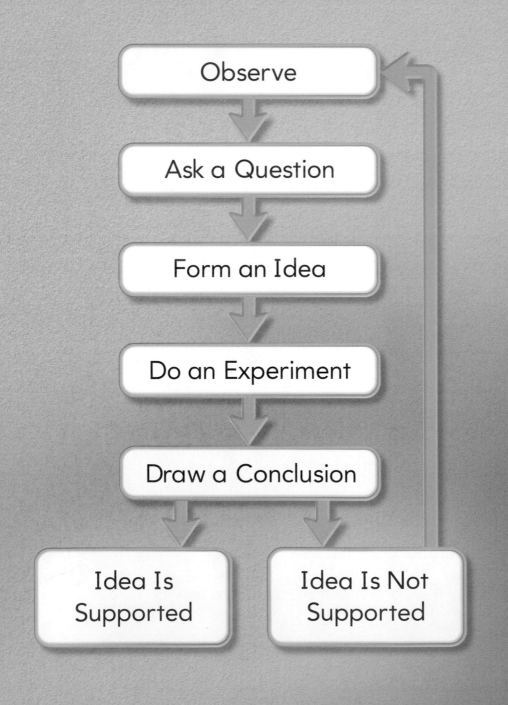

Observe

Ask a Question

Form an Idea

Do an Experiment

Draw a Conclusion

Idea Is Supported

Idea Is Not Supported

# Try it Yourself!

## Experiment With Bouncing Balls

Both balls look the same. However, one ball bounces and the other one does not.

 What questions do you have about the balls?

 How would you find out the answers?

 Write an experiment plan. Tell what you think you will find out.

# Be an Inventor

Lloyd French has enjoyed building things and taking them apart since sixth grade.

Mr. French invents robots. They are used as tools to make observations in places where people cannot easily go. One of his robots can travel to the bottom of the ocean. Another robot, called Cryobot, melts through thick layers of ice—either in Antarctica or on Mars. Cryobot takes photos as it moves through the ice.

**"If you want to be a scientist or engineer, it helps to have a sense of curiosity and discovery."**

# What Is Technology?

The tools people make and use are all **technology**. A pencil is technology. A cryobot is technology. So is a robot that moves like a human.

Scientists use technology. For example, a microscope makes it possible to see things that cannot be seen with just the eyes. Measurement tools are used to make their observations more exact.

Many technologies make the world a better place to live. But sometimes solving one problem causes others. For example, airplanes make travel faster, but they are noisy and pollute the air.

# A Better Idea

"I wish I had a better way to _____".
How would you fill in the blank?
Everyone wishes they could do something
more easily. Inventors try to make those
wishes come true. Inventing or improving
an invention takes time and patience.

Kids have been riding
on scooters for many
years. These newer
scooters are faster.
The tires won't get
flat. They are also
easier to carry from
place to place.

# How to Be an Inventor

1. **Find a problem.** It may be at school, at home, or in your community.

2. **Think of a way to solve the problem.** List different ways to solve the problem. Decide which one will work best.

3. **Make a sample and try your invention.** Your idea may need many materials or none at all. Each time you try it, record how it works.

4. **Improve your invention.** Use what you learned to make your design better.

5. **Share your invention.** Draw or write about your invention. Tell how it makes an activity easier or more fun. If it did not work well, tell why.

# Make Decisions

## Plastic Litter and Ocean Animals

It is a windy day at the beach. A plastic bag blows out of sight. It may float in the ocean for years.

Plastic litter can harm ocean animals. Sometimes sea turtles mistake floating plastic bags for jellyfish, their favorite food. The plastic blocks the stomach, and food cannot get in. Pelicans and dolphins get tangled up in fishing line, six-pack rings, and packaging materials. Sometimes they get so tangled that they cannot move.

# Deciding What to Do

How can ocean animals be protected from plastic litter?

Here's how to make your decision. You can use the same steps to help solve problems in your home, in your school, and in your community.

 **Learn** ▶ Learn about the problem. You could talk to an expert, read a science book, or explore a web site.

 **List** ▶ Make a list of actions you could take. Add actions other people could take.

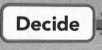 **Decide** ▶ Decide which action is best for you or your community.

**Share** ▶ Explain your decision to others.

# Science Safety

Know the safety rules of your classroom and follow them. Read and follow the safety tips in your science book.

- ▶ **Wear safety goggles when your teacher tells you.**

- ▶ **Keep your work area clean. Tell your teacher about spills right away.**

- ▶ **Learn how to care for the plants and animals in your classroom.**

- ▶ **Wash your hands when you are done.**

# LIFE SCIENCE

UNIT **B**

# Environments
## and Energy

**Cricket** Connection

Visit www.eduplace.com/scp/
to check out *Click, Ask,* and
*Odyssey* magazine articles
and activities.

# Environments and Energy

## Independent Reading

**Down by the Stream**

**River Otter**

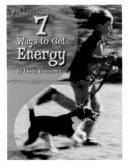

**7 Ways to Get Energy**

## Discover!

**Why are flamingos pink?**

**Think about this question as you read. You will have the answer by the end of the unit.**

# Crawdad Creek

by Scott Russell Sanders

illustrated by Robert Hynes

In the warm evenings, just before going in to bed, we sat very still beside Crawdad Creek, hoping to see the animals that made the tracks. And sure enough, we saw deer coming down to drink, saw rabbits nibbling and muskrats swimming, even saw raccoons grubbing for mussels in the water.

# Chapter 4

# Environments

environment
habitat
stream
woodland
resource
drought

### habitat

The part of an environment where a plant or an animal lives is its habitat.

### stream

A stream is a small river.

### woodland

A woodland is a place with many trees and bushes.

### drought

A long time with little or no rain is a drought.

# What Makes Up an Environment?

## Science and You

You can help living things survive when you know about environments.

## Inquiry Skill

**Classify** Sort organisms or objects into groups to show how they are alike.

### What You Need

hand lens

drawing paper

crayons

# Living or Nonliving

## Steps

STEP 1

1. **Observe** Look around a small rock or log for a living thing. Think about what it uses to meet its needs.

STEP 2

2. **Classify** Look up close. Decide whether each thing it uses is living or nonliving.

3. **Record Data** Make a chart like the one shown. Draw each thing you see in the correct place on the chart.

STEP 3

4. **Communicate** Show your chart to others. Talk about what you observed.

## Think and Share

1. Did your living thing use more living or nonliving things to meet its needs?

2. **Compare** How are the nonliving things alike?

## Investigate More!

**Ask Questions** Make a list of questions about the living things that you observed. Think of ways to find answers to your questions.

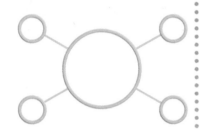

# Different Environments

All the living and nonliving things around a living thing make up an **environment**. Plants and animals are the living things. Soil, water, rocks, and air are some of the nonliving things.

The world has many kinds of environments. Different plants and animals live in each one. They adapt to the environment where they live.

**Alpine Tundra**

The alpine tundra is cold and dry. The plants grow low to the ground to be safe from the wind.

**Rain Forest**

A rain forest is a warm, wet forest with many kinds of plants.

An environment can be hot or cold. It can be wet or dry. Some environments have many trees and other plants. Other environments have very few plants.

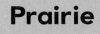 **MAIN IDEA** What are three different kinds of environments?

**Prairie**

The prairie is hot in summer and cold in winter.

In what kind of habitat does a fish need to live?

## Meeting Needs

Living things will survive only if they get what they need. So different plants and animals live in different environments. The part of an environment where a plant or an animal lives is its **habitat**.

In hot, desert habitats, animals find shade under rocks or under the ground. They look for food at night, when it is cooler. Many desert animals get water from the foods they eat.

Spotted skin helps the lizard blend in with its desert environment.

The thick stem of a cactus holds water.

◀ Hooves help mountain goats climb rocky slopes in the tundra.

Plants and animals have parts that help them live in their habitats. Some parts help them stay safe. Other parts help them get food and water.

A large beak helps a macaw crack open nuts it finds in the rain forest. ▼

▶ **MAIN IDEA** Why do different plants and animals live in different places?

## Lesson Wrap-Up

❶ **Vocabulary** What is a **habitat**?

❷ **Reading Skill** How do parts of plants and animals help them in their habitats?

❸ **Classify** Name two living things and two nonliving things in a desert.

**Technology** Visit **www.eduplace.com/scp/** to find out more about habitats.

# What Is a Stream Habitat?

## Science and You

Knowing about a stream habitat helps you know what living things you might find there.

## Inquiry Skill

**Use Models** You can use models to find out more about real things.

### What You Need

large pan

clay

rocks and pebbles

water

# Make a Stream

## Steps

1. **Use Models** Use clay to make a stream in a pan. Flatten the clay to make the bottom of the stream. Make walls of clay for the banks of the stream.

2. Put rocks and pebbles in the bottom of the stream.

3. **Observe** Slowly pour water in one end of the stream. Observe how the water moves.

## Think and Share

1. **Communicate** Describe the nonliving parts of a stream habitat.

2. **Infer** How might living things meet their needs in a stream habitat?

## Investigate More!

**Experiment** Plan ways to change how the water moves in your model stream. Record what happens each time. Share your results.

B13

## Learn by Reading

▶ **Vocabulary**
stream

▶ **Reading Skill**
Draw
Conclusions

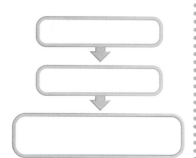

# A Stream Habitat

A **stream** is a small river. A stream and the area around it make up a stream habitat.

Many living and nonliving things are found in and around a stream. A stream habitat has plants and animals. It has air, water, rocks, and dirt. The water moves fast in some parts of the stream and more slowly in other parts.

**Water helps plants grow in and around a stream.**

Many living things meet their needs in a stream habitat. Plants and animals use water from the stream. They use the air around the stream. Fish move through the water. They eat plants and insects that live in the stream.

Raccoons use their senses to find crayfish and frogs along the banks of a stream.

▶ **DRAW CONCLUSIONS** What nonliving things in a stream habitat do animals use?

Rocks provide a place for small animals to hide.

# Life in a Stream

Living things in a stream habitat have adaptations to meet their needs. Plants that float have roots that hang in the water. A fish uses fins to swim. It uses gills to get air from the stream. A dragonfly uses its sense of sight to hunt for flying insects. A heron uses its long legs to walk in shallow water.

▶ **DRAW CONCLUSIONS** How does a turtle's shell help it in a stream habitat?

turtle

bass

minnow

dragonfly

heron

frog

## Lesson Wrap-Up

❶ **Vocabulary** What is a **stream**?

❷ **Reading Skill** How does a frog's color help it live in a stream habitat?

❸ **Use Models** How is using a model helpful?

🔦 **Technology** Visit **www.eduplace.com/scp/** to find out more about stream habitats.

# What Is a Woodland Habitat?

## Science and You

Knowing about a woodland habitat helps you understand the importance of trees.

## Inquiry Skill

**Use Models** You can use models to find out more about real things.

## What You Need

goggles

2 cups and tape

gravel, soil, and a spoon

moss or a fern and water

# Woodland Model

## Steps

 **Use Models**  Make a model of a woodland. Put some gravel in the bottom of a cup. Add soil until the cup is half full. **Safety:** Wear goggles!

② Spray the soil with water. Plant moss or a fern.

③ Put an empty cup on top of the first cup. Tape the cups together.

④ **Record Data**  Put your model in dim light. Record the changes you see each day.

STEP 1

STEP 2

STEP 3

## Think and Share

1. **Infer**  Why do you think a woodland model should be kept in dim light?

2. **Predict**  What changes do you think will happen over time?

## Investigate More!

**Experiment**  How might bright light affect your woodland model? Make and carry out a plan. Share what you observe.

**Vocabulary**

woodland

resource

**Reading Skill**

Compare and
Contrast

# A Woodland Habitat

A **woodland** is a place with many trees and bushes. Living things in a woodland have adaptations to help them survive. Small plants that live under tall trees can grow with less sunlight. Woodland animals use these plants for food and shelter.

Many woodland animals have body parts for climbing or flying to the tops of trees. The brown coloring of many woodland animals helps them to hide.

▶ **COMPARE AND CONTRAST** How are small plants different from tall trees in a woodland?

fox

hawk

squirrel

deer

skunk

pheasant

snake

B21

# Trees Are Resources

A **resource** is something that plants and animals use to live. A tree is a resource for woodland plants and animals. A tree can give living things food and shelter.

A woodpecker uses its beak to find insects inside a tree. ▶

Caterpillars get food and shelter from a tree's leaves.

**Both an owl and a squirrel use a tree for shelter.**

Animals use all parts of a tree. They use the roots, leaves, and nuts for food. Some animals build nests in tree branches. Others live on leaves or under the bark.

▶ **COMPARE AND CONTRAST** How do squirrels and caterpillars use trees in the same way?

## Lesson Wrap-Up

❶ **Vocabulary** What is a **resource**?

❷ **Reading Skill** Compare how a fox and a hawk are adapted to live in a woodland.

❸ **Use Models** What does a model show?

**Technology** Visit **www.eduplace.com/scp/** to find out more about woodland habitats.

# Creating Habitats

Aquariums and zoos have habitats made by people. Workers study living things in the real habitats. Then they build the habitats indoors.

The Tennessee Aquarium has indoor woodland and stream habitats. The streams are made of long tanks of water. Computers keep the woodland air cool and wet. They also control the flow of water in the streams.

**A pointed glass roof at the Tennessee Aquarium lets in sunlight.** ▼

The plants in the Appalachian Cove Forest grow and change as if they were in a real woodland.

## Sharing Ideas

1. **Write About It**  How does the Tennessee Aquarium use technology to make woodland and stream habitats?

2. **Talk About It**  Why do you think aquarium workers spend time studying habitats?

B25

# How Do Environments Change?

## Science and You

You can help care for environments by knowing how they change.

## Inquiry Skill

**Predict** Use what you know and observe to tell what you think will happen.

2 cups of grass

tray

water

2 craft sticks

# Predict Change

## Steps

1. Write **Water** on one stick. Write **No Water** on the other stick. Label each cup of grass. Water only the grass labeled **Water**.

STEP 1

2. **Predict** Place the cups on a tray in a sunny window. Tell how you think each cup of grass might change after five days.

STEP 2

3. Continue to water only the grass labeled **Water** each day for five days. Record your results.

STEP 3

## Think and Share

1. **Infer** How did each cup of grass change? Tell why.

2. **Compare** How did your results compare to your prediction?

## Investigate More!

**Experiment** Plan a way to find out what happens when a plant gets too much water. Carry out your plan. Share the results with your classmates.

**Vocabulary**

drought

**Reading Skill**

Cause and
Effect

# Nature Changes Environments

Things that happen in nature
can change an environment. The
changes can be slow or fast. They
can be harmful or helpful. Forest
fires harm trees. But the fires help
some seeds grow into new trees.

Too much rain can cause a flood.
A long time with little or no rain is
a **drought**. Without water, plants
cannot grow. Animals do not get
enough to eat and drink. Plants
and animals might die.

effect of drought ▶

Plants also can change an environment. New plants might block sunlight needed by other plants. Animals that depend on these plants must find other things to eat.

Some animals might harm the resources of other animals. The animals then must find new homes or new kinds of food. Other animals might help the environment by making new habitats.

▶ **CAUSE AND EFFECT** How can a drought change an environment?

▲ **Kudzu is a vine that can kill trees by blocking the sunlight.**

A beaver builds a dam, and a pond forms behind it. The pond is a new home for many animals.

# Animals Adapt to Change

People can change an environment by building in places where plants and animals live. Animals can learn to adapt to their changed habitats. Instead of finding food in a woodland, an animal might find food in household trash.

**This skunk has learned to meet its needs in a changed environment.**

## Lesson Wrap-Up

❶ **Vocabulary** What is a time of little rain called?

❷ **Reading Skill** What can cause an environment to change?

❸ **Predict** What might happen to a vegetable garden if no rain fell for a long time?

**Technology** Visit **www.eduplace.com/scp/** to find out more about how environments change.

## Math | Use a Bar Graph

Ms. Park's class observed the trees near their school. The graph shows how many different trees they saw.

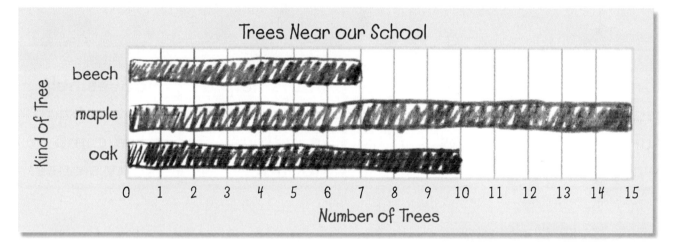

Trees Near our School

Kind of Tree: beech, maple, oak
Number of Trees: 0 1 2 3 4 5 6 7 8 9 10 11 12 13 14 15

1. How many oak and beech trees are there altogether?

2. How many more maple trees are there than beech trees?

## Social Studies | Make a Poster

Think about how you meet your needs in your habitat. Make a poster to show how you meet one of those needs.

I get food at a grocery store.

## Visual Summary

Animals have features that help them live in their environments.

| Stream | Woodland | Desert | Tundra |
|---|---|---|---|
| Fins help a fish swim through water. | Claws help a squirrel climb trees. | Spots help a lizard blend in with its habitat. | Hooves help a mountain goat climb rocky slopes. |

## Main Ideas

1. Describe what makes up an environment. (p. B8)

2. How do fish use a stream to meet their needs? (pp. B14–B16)

3. How do animals use trees to meet their needs? (pp. B22–B23)

4. What events in nature can change an environment? (pp. B28–B29)

## Vocabulary

**Choose the correct word from the box.**

5. A long time with little or no rain

6. A place with many trees and bushes

7. The part of an environment where a plant or an animal lives

8. Something that plants and animals use to live

| |
|---|
| **habitat** (p. B10) |
| **woodland** (p. B20) |
| **resource** (p. B22) |
| **drought** (p. B28) |

## Test Practice

**Choose a word to complete the sentence.**

9. A _____ is a small river.

    shelter    woodland    drought    stream

## Using Science Skills

10. **Classify** Draw a picture of three animals in a stream habitat. Draw another picture of three animals in a woodland habitat. Compare your drawings.

11. **Critical Thinking** Why do people need to be careful about where they build new buildings?

# Chapter 5

# Energy Needs

energy
food chain
food web
healthful food
healthful meal

**energy**

Energy is the ability to do things.

**food chain**

A food chain is the order in which energy passes from one living thing to another.

**healthful food**

A healthful food is a food that is good for your body.

**healthful meal**

A healthful meal is a meal with foods from the different food groups.

# How Do Plants and Animals Get Energy?

## Science and You

Knowing about food chains helps you understand how living things depend on their environments.

## Inquiry Skill

Use Models You can use models to find out more about real things.

## What You Need

food chain strips

scissors

glue

# Make a Food Chain

## Steps

**STEP 1**

1. Cut along the dotted lines to make food chain strips.
**Safety:** Scissors are sharp!

2. Find the strip with the Sun. Glue the ends together to make a loop.

**STEP 2**

3. **Use Models** Add loops in the correct order to make a food chain. Use the clues on the strips.

4. **Communicate** Talk with a partner. Tell how each link connects to the next link.

**STEP 3**

## Think and Share

1. Why did your food chain model start with the Sun?

2. Why does a hawk need plants to live?

## Investigate More!

**Ask Questions** Ask about what some other animals eat. Use what you learn to make a new food chain.

# Food and Energy

When you run, play a game, or clean your room, you use energy. **Energy** is the ability to do things. <u>Living things get the energy they need from food.</u>

Remember that plants are living things. Plants use sunlight to make their own food. The food gives them energy to grow and change.

**Young wasps get energy by eating part of a hornworm.**

Animals are living things, too. Animals get energy to grow and change from the food they eat. Different animals eat different kinds of food. Some animals eat only plants. Some eat only other animals. Some animals eat both plants and other animals.

▶ **SEQUENCE** What do animals do to get energy?

▲ Spiders hunt and eat insects.

Giraffes eat only plants. ▶

## Food Chains

A chain is made of parts that are linked in some way. <u>Plants and animals are linked by the energy they use to live.</u> A **food chain** shows the order in which energy passes from one living thing to another.

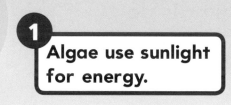

**1** Algae use sunlight for energy.

**2** A small fish eats the algae.

Almost all food chains start with the Sun. Most plants get energy by turning sunlight into food. The arrows show the direction that energy moves in each food chain.

▶ **SEQUENCE** With what do most food chains begin?

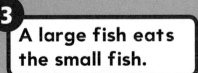

**3** A large fish eats the small fish.

**1** Grass gets energy from the Sun.

**2** A cow eats the grass.

**3** A child drinks milk that came from the cow.

red-tailed hawk

cactus mouse

grama grass

## Food Webs

Many food chains can be found at the same time in one environment. A **food web** shows how different food chains are related. The picture shows a food web made up of some desert food chains.

One part of a food web may change. When this happens, the lives of other living things in the web can change, too.

▶ **SEQUENCE** Tell the order in which energy moves from the Sun to a rattlesnake.

rattlesnake

jackrabbit

## Lesson Wrap-Up

1. **Vocabulary** What is **energy**?

2. **Reading Skill** What is one way that energy moves from the Sun to a hawk?

3. **Use Models** What does a food chain show?

**Technology** Visit **www.eduplace.com/scp/** to find out more about food chains and food webs.

Parts of a story about life in and around an Alaskan river are shown. Look for food chains as you read.

# River of Life

by Debbie S. Miller
illustrated by Jon Van Zyle

Salmon fry swim in quiet pools that are shaded by the trees. They eat plankton and tiny insects. *Splash, slip.*

A kingfisher sends its loud rattling call above the river. He wears a bluish-gray feathered crest. He catches wiggly salmon with a beak that looks too long for his head. Beneath the surface, a rainbow trout chases salmon fry. The trout catches a glimpse of something shiny. Will it take a bite?

## Sharing Ideas

1. **Write About It** Draw a food chain or food web described in the story. Be sure to label its parts.
2. **Talk About It** What animals might eat trout from the river?

# How Do People Get Energy?

## Science and You

Eating the right kinds of foods helps you play, learn, and grow.

## Inquiry Skill

Classify Sort objects into groups to show how they are alike.

### What You Need

food ads

paper

scissors

glue

# Classify Foods

## Steps

**1** **Compare** Look at food ads. Look for foods that are alike. Look for foods that are different.

**2** Cut out pictures of 10 different foods. **Safety:** Scissors are sharp!

**3** **Classify** Fold a sheet of paper into four parts. Sort the pictures into four groups. Glue each group to a different part of the paper.

STEP 1

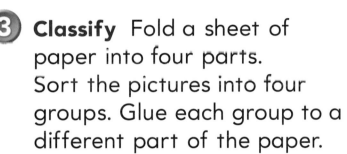

STEP 2

STEP 3

## Think and Share

1. **Communicate** Tell how you sorted the foods.

2. What other ways could the foods be sorted?

## Investigate More!

**Work Together** Survey classmates to find out what foods they do not like. Discuss as a group how the foods named in the survey are alike.

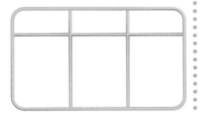

# People Get Energy from Food

People are living things that need food, air, water, and shelter. <u>Food gives people the energy needed to do everyday things.</u>

Foods come from different places. Think about foods you see at a market or grocery store. They all come from somewhere else.

**Farmers grow vegetables in soil.**

**Farmers gather eggs from chickens.**

A farmer grows vegetables and a fisher catches fish. A grocer buys the vegetables and fish from the farmer and the fisher. Then the grocer sells these foods to the shoppers.

▶ **CLASSIFY** Where might grocers get the food they sell?

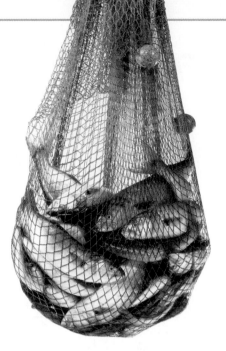

▲ Fish come from rivers, lakes, and oceans.

Where do the vegetables in this market come from? ▼

## Food Choices

Some foods are better for you than others. A **healthful food** is a food that is good for your body. Healthful foods give your body energy and vitamins. Healthful foods can be sorted into groups. <u>Eating healthful foods from each group helps your body be its best.</u>

Foods such as candy and other sweets are not as good for you. These foods will not help your body be its best. Be sure to eat healthful foods most of the time.

▶ **CLASSIFY** Which foods help your body be its best?

**In which food groups do the cereal and the lettuce belong?**

grains: bread, cereal, rice, pasta

milk: milk, cheese, yogurt

meat and beans: meat, chicken, fish, eggs, beans, nuts

vegetables

fruits

# Healthful Meals

It is important to eat healthful foods at each meal and as snacks. A **healthful meal** is a meal with foods from the different food groups.

**❶ Vocabulary** What is an example of a **healthful food**?

**❷ Reading Skill** Name two foods that come from a farm.

**❸ Classify** Which two foods belong in the same group?

**Technology** Visit **www.eduplace.com/scp/** to find out more about food and energy.

## Math Read a Chart

This chart shows the favorite healthful foods of children in a second-grade class.

| Healthful Foods | |
| --- | --- |
| Favorite Food | Number of Children |
| apples | 5 |
| carrots | 1 |
| pasta | 3 |
| cheese | 4 |

1. Cheese is the favorite food of how many?

2. How many children have a favorite food that is a fruit or vegetable?

## Language Arts Food Chain Book

Make a picture book about a food chain. Find out about a food chain on your own, or use one of these food chains.

**fruit, fly, spider, lizard**

**leaf, caterpillar, frog, snake**

**arrow worm, herring, salmon, shark**

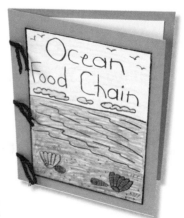

## Visual Summary

Living things need energy from food to live.

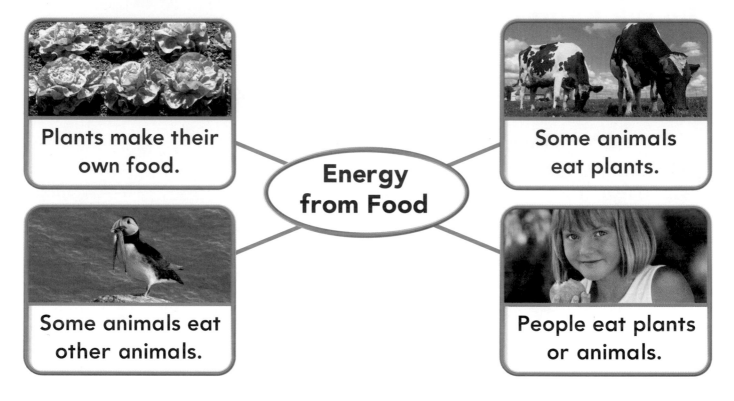

Plants make their own food.

Energy from Food

Some animals eat plants.

Some animals eat other animals.

People eat plants or animals.

## Main Ideas

1. Describe how plants and animals get energy. **(pp. B38–B39)**

2. What starts each food chain? **(p. B41)**

3. How is a food chain different from a food web? **(pp. B40–B43)**

4. How do people meet their need for energy? **(p. B48)**

## Vocabulary

**Choose the correct word from the box.**

5. A food that is good for your body

6. The ability to do things

7. Meal with foods from the different food groups

8. The order in which energy passes from one living thing to another

| |
|---|
| **energy** (p. B38) |
| **food chain** (p. B40) |
| **healthful food** (p. B50) |
| **healthful meal** (p. B52) |

## ✓ Test Practice

**Choose a word to complete the sentence.**

9. A _____ shows how different food chains are related.

food group    food web    market    meal

## ✏ Using Science Skills

10. **Classify** List three foods that belong in the same group. Tell why.

11. **Critical Thinking** What might happen to a food web if all of the plants died?

**Discover!**

## Why are flamingos pink?

Flamingos are pink because of a food chain. Flamingos eat animals called crustaceans. Crustaceans eat algae. Algae contain nutrients that can cause things to be pink. When a flamingo eats the crustaceans, it takes in these nutrients. This causes the flamingo's feathers to turn pink.

Go to **www.eduplace.com/scp/** to study more animal food chains.

# Science and Math Toolbox

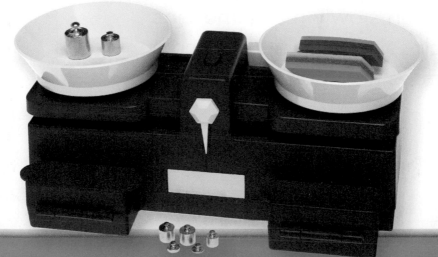

# Using a Hand Lens

A hand lens is a tool that makes objects look bigger. It helps you see the small parts of an object.

## Look at a Coin

**1** Place a coin on your desk.

STEP 1

**2** Hold the hand lens above the coin. Look through the lens. Slowly move the lens away from the coin. What do you see?

**3** Keep moving the lens away until the coin looks blurry.

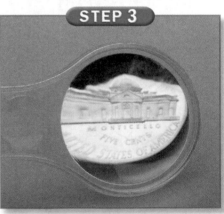

STEP 3

**4** Then slowly move the lens closer. Stop when the coin does not look blurry.

STEP 4

# Using a Thermometer

A thermometer is a tool used to measure temperature. Temperature tells how hot or cold something is. It is measured in degrees.

## Find the Temperature of Water

 Put water into a cup.

 Put a thermometer into the cup.

 Watch the colored liquid in the thermometer. What do you see?

 Look how high the colored liquid is. What number is closest? That is the temperature of the water.

# Using a Ruler

A ruler is a tool used to measure the length of objects. Rulers measure length in inches or centimeters.

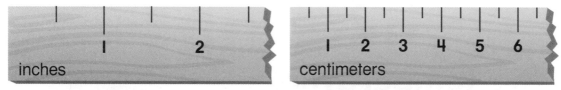

**inches**                    **centimeters**

## Measure a Crayon

**1** Place the ruler on your desk.

**2** Lay your crayon next to the ruler. Line up one end with the end of the ruler.

**3** Look at the other end of the crayon. Which number is closest to that end?

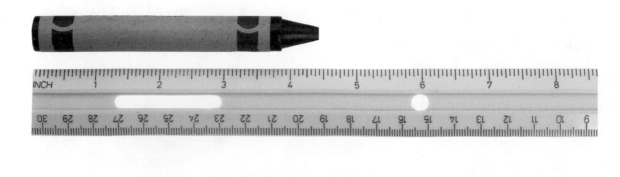

# Using a Calculator

A calculator is a tool that can help you add and subtract numbers.

## Subtract Numbers

**1** Tim and Anna grew plants. Tim grew 5 plants. Anna grew 8 plants.

**2** How many more plants did Anna grow? Use your calculator to find out.

**3** Enter 8 on the calculator. Then press the − key. Enter 5 and press = .

## What is your answer?

Tim's Plants

Anna's Plants

# Using a Balance

A balance is a tool used to measure mass. Mass is the amount of matter in an object.

## Compare the Mass of Objects

 Check that the pointer is on the middle mark of the balance. If needed, move the slider on the back to the left or right.

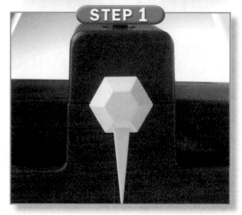

STEP 1

2 Place a clay ball in one pan. Place a crayon in the other pan.

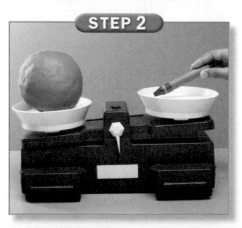

STEP 2

3 Observe the positions of the two pans.

**Does the clay ball or the crayon have more mass?**

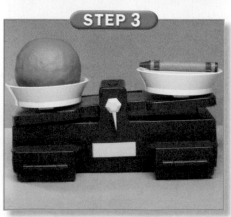

STEP 3

# Making a Chart

A chart can help you sort information, or data. When you sort data it is easier to read and compare.

## Make a Chart to Compare Animals

**1** Give the chart a title.

**2** Name the groups that tell about the data you collect. Label the columns with the names.

**3** Carefully fill in the data in each column.

**Which animal can move in the most ways?**

### How Animals Move

| Animal | How it Moves |
|--------|--------------|
| fish | swim |
| dog | walk, swim |
| duck | walk, fly, swim |

# Making a Tally Chart

A tally chart helps you keep track of items as you count.

## Make a Tally Chart of Kinds of Pets

Jan's class made a tally chart to record the number of each kind of pet they own.

1. Every time they counted one pet, they made one tally.

2. When they got to five, they made the fifth tally a line across the other four.

3. Count the tallies to find each total.

**How many of each kind of pet do the children have?**

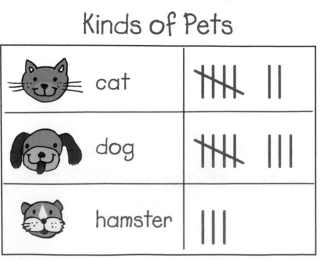

Kinds of Pets

| | | |
|---|---|---|
| 🐱 | cat | 卌 \|\| |
| 🐶 | dog | 卌 \|\|\| |
| 🐹 | hamster | \|\|\| |

# Making a Bar Graph

A bar graph can help you sort and compare data.

## Make a Bar Graph of Favorite Pets

You can use the data in the tally chart on page H8 to make a bar graph.

1 Choose a title for your graph.

2 Write numbers along the side.

3 Write pet names along the bottom.

4 Start at the bottom of each column. Fill in one box for each tally.

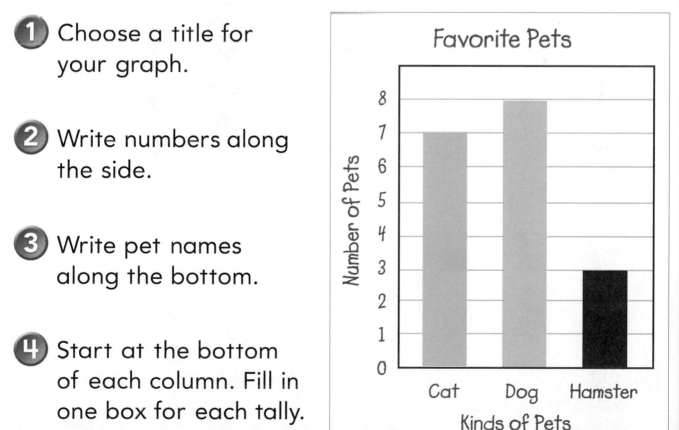

Which pet is the favorite?

# Health and Fitness Handbook

When your body works well, you are healthy.
Here are some ways to stay healthy.

- Know how your body works.

- Follow safety rules.

- Dance, jump, run, or swim to make
  your body stronger.

- Eat foods that give your body what
  it needs.

# Your Senses

Your five senses help you learn about the world. They help you stay safe.

## Sight

Light enters the eye through the pupil. The iris controls how much light comes in. Other parts of the eye turn the light into messages that go to the brain.

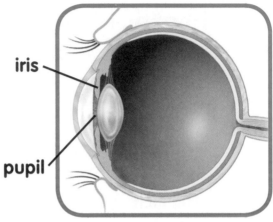

The iris is the colored part of the eye.

## Hearing

The ear has three main parts. Most of your ear is inside your head. Sound makes some parts of the ear move back and forth very fast. The inner ear sends information about the sound to the brain.

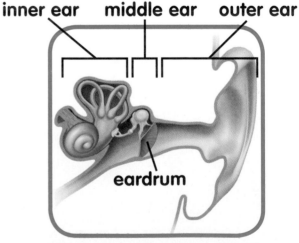

The eardrum is easily injured. Never stick anything in your ear.

## Taste

Your tongue is covered with thousands of tiny bumps called taste buds. They help you taste sweet, salty, sour, and bitter things. Some parts of the tongue seem to sense some flavors more strongly. The whole tongue tastes salty foods.

bitter

sour — — sour

sweet

Your body makes a new set of taste buds about every two weeks.

## Smell

All kinds of smells travel through the air. These smells enter your nose. Your nose sends messages to your brain about them.

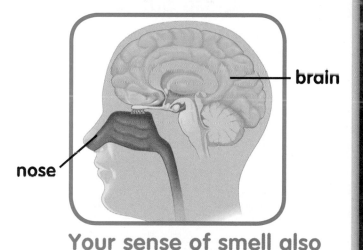

brain

nose

Your sense of smell also helps you taste.

## Touch

Touch a tree trunk, and it feels rough. A kitten feels soft. Your skin senses all this information. Then the brain decides how to respond.

Your skin is your body's largest organ.

# Protect Eyes and Ears

You use your eyes and ears to see and hear. You can protect your eyes and ears.

## Protect Your Eyes

- Keep sharp things away from your eyes.

- Wear sunglasses when you are outside. They protect your eyes from the Sun's rays.

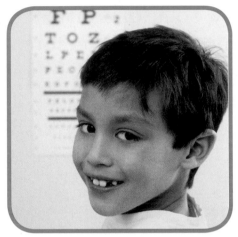

An eye test can help tell if a person needs glasses.

## Protect Your Ears

- Wear a helmet when you play baseball or softball.

- Loud noises can damage your ears. Keep music at a low volume.

A hearing test tells if a person has a hearing loss.

# Staying Safe on the Road

How do you get to school or a playground? Here are ways to help you stay safe.

## Walk Safely

- Stay on the sidewalk.

- Walk with a friend or trusted adult.

- Cross at crosswalks. Look both ways before you cross!

- Don't run between parked cars. Drivers might not see you.

Only cross when the "walk" sign is lit.

Obey crossing guards.

## Car and Bus Safety

- If a bus has seat belts, wear one.

- Stay seated and talk quietly so the driver can pay attention to the road.

- Cross the street in front of a bus after all traffic stops.

Always wear your seat belt in a car.

# Move Your Muscles!

All kinds of things can be exercise. Here are some ways you can make your muscles stronger.

## By Yourself

- Kick a ball as far as you can. Chase it and kick it back.
- Ride your bike.
- Jump rope.
- Do jumping jacks.
- Put on music and dance.

## With Others

- Play ball!
- Play tag. Run!
- Go for a hike.
- Play hopscotch.
- Play with a flying disk.

# Food Groups

Food gives your body energy and what your body needs to grow. Foods in different groups help you in different ways.

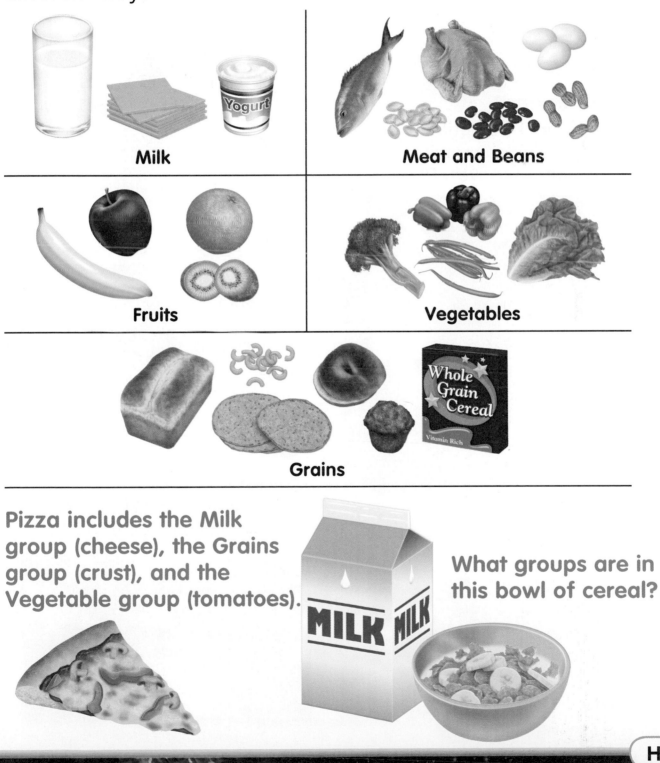

Milk

Meat and Beans

Fruits

Vegetables

Grains

**Pizza includes the Milk group (cheese), the Grains group (crust), and the Vegetable group (tomatoes).**

**What groups are in this bowl of cereal?**

# Picture Glossary

### A

**adaptation**

A body part or action that helps a living thing meet its needs where it lives. (A54)

**amphibian**

An animal that lives part of its life in water and part of its life on land. (A44)

**ask questions**

Learn more about what you observe by asking questions of yourself and others.

**attracts**

When a magnet pulls an object toward itself. (F38)

### B

**bird**

An animal that has feathers and wings. (A38)

### C

**classify**

Sort objects into groups that are alike in some way.

## communicate

Share what you learn with others by talking, drawing pictures, or making charts and graphs.

## compare

Look for ways that objects or events are alike or different.

## condenses

Changes from water vapor to drops of water. (D11)

## cone

Part of a nonflowering plant where seeds form. (A20)

## conserve

To use less of something to make it last longer. (C50)

## constellation

A group of stars that forms a picture. (D58)

 **D**

## dissolves

Mixes completely with water. (E17)

## drought

A long time with little or no rain. (B28)

# E

### echo
A sound that repeats when sound waves bounce off a surface. (E47)

### energy
The ability to do things. Living things get energy from food. (B38)

### environment
All of the living and nonliving things around a living thing. (B8)

### erosion
The carrying of weathered rock and soil from place to place. (C18)

### evaporates
Changes to a gas. The Sun warms water, and water evaporates. (D10)

### experiment
Make a plan to collect data and then share the results with others.

| Testing Magnets | |
|---|---|
| Position of the Magnets | What Happened |
| | |

# F

### fibrous root
A root that has many thin branches. (A22)

## fish
An animal that lives in water and has gills. (A46)

## food web
A model that shows how different food chains are related. (B42)

## flower
The plant part where fruit and seeds form. (A14)

## force
A push or a pull. (F14)

## food chain
The order in which energy passes from one living thing to another. (B40)

## fossil
Something that remains of a living thing from long ago. (C22)

## friction
A force that makes an object slow down when it rubs against another object. (F16)

**fruit**
The part of a flower that grows around a seed. (A14)

**healthful food**
A food that is good for your body. (B50)

**G**

**gas**
A state of matter that spreads out to fill a space. A gas fills the inside of a balloon. (E11)

**healthful meal**
A meal with foods from the different food groups. (B52)

**gravity**
A pull toward the center of Earth. Objects fall to the ground unless something holds them up. (C18, F11)

**hibernate**
To go into a deep sleep. (D27)

**H**

**habitat**
The part of an environment where a plant or an animal lives. (B10)

**humus**
Tiny bits of dead plants and animals in soil. (C10)

## imprint
The shape of a living thing found in rock. (C22)

## infer
Use what you observe and know to tell what you think.

## larva
A wormlike thing that hatches from an egg. (A74)

## lever
A bar that moves around a fixed point. (F27)

## life cycle
The series of changes that a living thing goes through as it grows. (A26)

## liquid
A state of matter that does not have its own shape. (E10)

## litter
Trash on the ground. (C45)

**living thing**
Something that grows and changes. (A8)

**magnify**
To make objects look larger. (E26)

**magnetic**
An object that is attracted to a magnet. (F42)

**mammal**
An animal that has fur or hair and makes milk to feed its young. (A36)

**magnetic field**
The area around a magnet where the magnet's force acts. (F50)

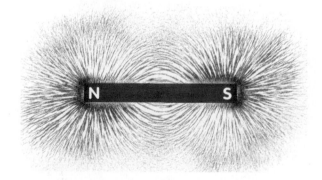

**mass**
The amount of matter in an object. You can measure mass with a balance. (E13)

**measure**
Use different tools to collect data about the properties of objects.

**migrate**
To move to warmer places in fall. (D27)

**mineral**
A nonliving solid found in nature. One or more minerals form rocks. (C8)

**mixture**
Something made of two or more things. (E16)

**Moon**
A large sphere made of rock. (D48)

**motion**
Moving from one place to another. (F10)

 **N**

**natural resource**
Something found in nature that people need or use. (C34)

### nonmagnetic
An object that is not attracted to a magnet. (F43)

### nutrient
A material in soil that helps a plant live and grow. Roots take in water and nutrients from the soil. (A11)

### offspring
The group of living things that come from the same living thing. (A64)

### orbit
The path that one space object travels around another. (D44)

## P

### phases
The different ways the moon looks. (D50)

## O

### observe
Use tools and the senses to learn about the properties of an object or event.

### pitch
How high or low a sound is. Cymbals have a low pitch. (E50)

**planet**
A large object that moves around the Sun. (D38)

**pole**
The place on a magnet where the force is the strongest. (F37)

**pollution**
Waste that harms the land, water, or air. (C45)

**position**
A place or location. The bird is on top of the cactus. (F8)

**precipitation**
Water that falls from clouds. (D12)

**predict**
Use what you know and patterns you observe to tell what will happen.

| Testing Objects | | |
|---|---|---|
| Object | Prediction | What Happened |
| | | |
| | | |
| | | |
| | | |
| | | |

**properties**
Color, shape, size, odor, and texture. A penny is small and round. (E8)

**pulley**
A wheel with a groove through which a rope or chain moves. (F28)

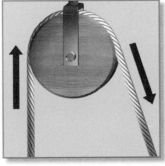

**pupa**
The stage between larva and adult when an insect changes form. (A75)

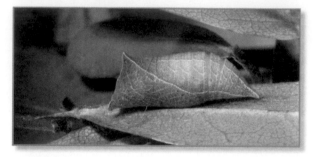

**ramp**
A slanted tool used to move things from one level to another. (F26)

**record data**
Write or draw to show what you have observed.

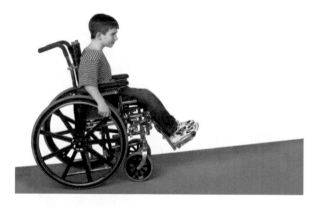

**recycle**
To collect items made of materials that can be used to make new items. (C50)

**repels**
When a magnet pushes an object away from itself. (F39)

**reproduce**
To make more living things of the same kind. (A64)

**reptile**
An animal whose skin is covered with dry scales. (A42)

**resource**
Something that plants and animals use to live. (B22)

**reuse**
To use again and again. Old tires can be reused on a playground. (C52)

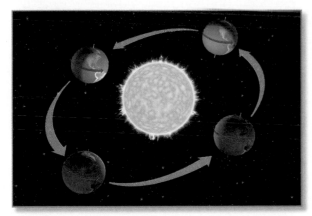

**revolve**
To move in a path around an object. (D44)

**rock**
A solid made of one or more minerals. (C8)

**rotates**
Spins around an imaginary line. (D42)

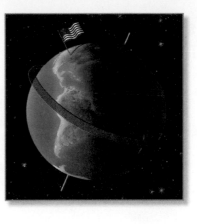

 **S**

**season**
A time of year. (D16)

**seed**
The part from which a new plant grows. (A14)

**seedling**
A young plant that grows from a seed. (A26)

### separate
To take apart. (E16)

### shelter
A place where a living thing can be safe. (A9)

### simple machine
A tool that can make it easier to move objects. (F26)

### soil
The loose material that covers Earth's surface. (C10)

### solar system
The Sun and the space objects that move around it. (D38)

### solid
A state of matter that has its own size and shape. (E10)

### sound
Energy that you hear. (E36)

### sound wave
Vibrating air. (E38)

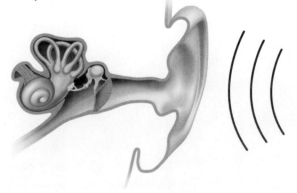

### star
A big ball of hot gases that gives off light. (D56)

### stream
A small river. (B14)

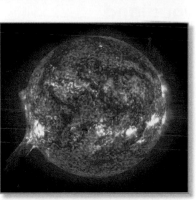

### Sun
The brightest object in the day sky. (D36)

### T

### taproot
A root that has one main branch. (A22)

### U

### use data
Use what you observe and record to find patterns and make predictions.

### use models
Use something like the real thing to understand how the real thing works.

### use numbers
Count, measure, order, or estimate to describe and compare objects and events.

| Length of Triops | |
|---|---|
| Day 1 | about _____ cm |
| Day 2 | about _____ cm |
| Day 3 | about _____ cm |
| Day 4 | about _____ cm |
| Day 5 | about _____ cm |

## V

### vibrates

Moves back and forth very fast. A guitar string vibrates to make a sound. (E36)

### volume

1. The amount of space a liquid takes up. (E12)

2. How loud or soft a sound is. A siren is loud. (E51)

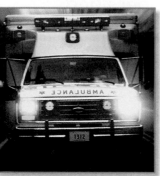

## W

### water cycle

Water moving from Earth to the air and back again. (D10)

### water vapor

Water as a gas. You cannot see water vapor. (D10)

### weathering

The wearing away and breaking apart of rock. (C16)

### woodland

A place with many trees and bushes. (B20)

### work together

Work as a group to share ideas, data, and observations.

Index

**Index**

Credits

## Permission Acknowledgements

Excerpt from The Tale of Rabbit and Coyote, by Tony Johnston, illustrated by Tomie de Paola. Text copyright © 1998 by Roger D. Johnston and Susan T. Johnston as Trustees of the Johnston Family Trust. Illustrations copyright © 1998 by Tomie de Paola. Used by permission of G.P. Putnam's Sons, a Division of Penguin Young Readers Group, A Member of Penguin Group (USA) Inc., 345 Hudson Street, New York, NY 10014, the author and Writers House LLC, acting as agent for the author. All rights reserved. Excerpt from Motion: Push and Pull, Fast and Slow, by Darlene Stille, illustrated by Sheree Boyd. Copyright © 2004 by Picture Window Books. Reprinted by permission of Picture Window Books. Excerpt from Let's Go Rock Collecting, by Roma Gans, illustrated by Holly Keller. Text copyright © 1984, 1997 by Roma Gans. Illustrations copyright © 1997 by Holly Keller. Reprinted by permission of HarperCollins Publishers. Excerpt from From Seed to Pumpkin, by Wendy Pfeffer, illustrated by James Graham Hale. Text copyright © 2004 by Wendy Pfeffer. Illustrations copyright © 2004 by James Graham Hale. Reprinted by permission of HarperCollins Publishers. Excerpt from River of Life, by Debbie S. Miller, illustrated by Jon Van Zyle. Text copyright © 2000 by Debbie S. Miller. Illustrations copyright © 2000 by Jon Van Zyle. Reprinted by permission of Clarion Books, an imprint of Houghton Mifflin Company. Excerpt from Crawdad Creek, by Scott Russell Sanders, illustrated by Robert Hynes. Text copyright © 1999 by Scott Russell Sanders. Illustrations copyright © 1999 by Robert Hynes. Reprinted by permission of National Geographic Society. Excerpt from The Starry Sky: The Sun and Moon, by Patrick Moore, illustrated by Paul Doherty. Copyright © 1994 Aladdin Books Limited. Text copyright © 1994 by Patrick Moore. Revised edition © 2000. Reprinted by permission of Aladdin Books Limited. Excerpt from The Sun: Our Nearest Star, by Franklyn M. Branley, illustrated by Edward Miller. Text copyright © 1961, 1988, 2002 by Franklyn M. Branley. Illustrations copyright © 2002 by Edward Miller III. Reprinted by permission of HarperCollins Publishers. Excerpt from My House's Night Song from My House is Singing, by Betsy R. Rosenthal. Copyright © 2004 by Betsy R. Rosenthal. Reprinted by permission of Harcourt, Inc. This material may not be reproduced in any form or by any means without the prior written permission of the publisher. *Wind Song* from *I Feel The Same Way*, by Lilian Moore. Copyright © 1967, 1995 by Lilian Moore. Reprinted by permission of Marian Reiner Literary Agency.
Excerpt from What's the Matter in Mr. Whisker's Room, by Michael Elsohn Ross, illustrated by Paul Meisel. Text copyright © 2004 by Michael Elsohn Ross. Illustrations copyright © 2004 by Paul Meisel. Reproduced by permission of the publisher Candlewick Press Inc., Cambridge, MA.

## Cover

(bear cub) (Spine) Daniel J. Cox/Getty Images.(Back cover bears) Tom Walker/Getty Images. (landscape) Panoramic Images/Getty Images.

## Photography

Unit A Opener Martin Harvey/Wild Images. **A1** Dave Watts/Dave Watts Photography. **A4–A5** Robert W. Ginn/Photo Edit, Inc. **A5** (tc) Colin Keates/DK Images. (bc) © Dwight Kuhn. (t) Gary VestalPhotographer's Choice/Getty Images. **A6** (bl) Robert A. Ross/Color Pic, Inc. **A6–A7** (bkgd) Andrew Brown/Ecoscene/Corbis. **A9** (tr) Bob & Clara Calhoun/ Bruce Coleman, Inc. (br) Jeff Foott/Bruce Coleman, Inc. **A10** (inset) Nigel Cattlin/Photo Researchers, Inc. **A10–A11** (bkgd) Michael Busselle/ Taxi/Getty Images. **A12–A13** (bkgd) Kathy Atkinson/Osf/Animals Animals. **A14** (l) Philip Dowell/DK Images. (r) © Dwight Kuhn. **A16** (t) Photo 24/Brand X Pictures/Getty Images. (b) N. Et Perennou/Photo Researchers, Inc. **A17** (t) M. Loup/Peter Arnold. (b) Matthew Ward/DK Images. **A18** (b) Alan & Linda Detrick/Photo Researchers, Inc. **A18–A19** (bkgd) Adam Jones/Osf/Animals Animals. **A20** (c) Matthew Ward/DK Images. (b) Colin Keates/DK Images. **A21** (tl) William Leonard/DRK Photo. **A21** (tr), (bl), (br) Matthew Ward/Dk Images. A22 (tl), (tr) © Dwight Kuhn. **A23** (tl) Ace Stock/Alamy Images. (r) Lani Howe/Photri. (bl) Jan Stromme/Bruce Coleman, Inc. **A24–A25** (bkgd) Michael B. Gadomski/Photo Researchers, Inc. **A28** (tr) © Dwight Kuhn. **A30** (l)© E.R. Degginger/Color–Pic, Inc. (lc) M. Loup/Peter Arnold. (c) © Dwight Kuhn. (rc) Colin Keates/DK Images. (r) Matthew Ward/DK Images. **A32–A33** (bkgd) Stephen J. Krasemann/DRK Photo. **A33** (t) Brain Stablyk/ Photographer's Choice/Getty Images. (tc) Skip Moody/Dembinsky Photo Associates. (bc) John Cancalosi/DRK Photo. **A33** (b) G. Staebler/ Masterfile. **A34–A35** (bkgd) Leslie Newman & Andrew Flowers/Photo Researchers, Inc. **A36** Brian Stablyk/Photographer's Choice/Getty Images. A37 (cl) Alan & Sandy Carey/Photo Researchers, Inc. (br) Tom Brakefield/DRK Photo. **A38** (t) K. McGougan/Bruce Coleman, Inc. (bl) Skip Moody/Dembinsky Photo Associates. **A39** Norman Owen Tomalin/ Bruce Coleman, Inc. **A40** (bl) Frans Lantig/Minden Pictures. **A40–A41** (bkgd) Maresa Pryor/Earth Scenes/Animals Animals. **A42** Rod Planck/ Photo Researchers, Inc. **A43** (tr) John Cancalosi/DRK Photo. (b) S.Gatzen/EyePress/Photri. **A44** (r) Sharon Cummings/Dembinsky Photo Associates. (bl) Gay Bumgarner/Index Stock Imagery. (frog) Skip Moody/ Dembinsky Photo Associates. **A45** (tr) Frans Lanting/Minden Pictures. (tl) Michael & Patricia Fogden/Minden Pictures. (cr) Scott Camazine/Photo Researchers, Inc. (b) Dwight Kuhn/Bruce Coleman, Inc. **A46** (tl) William Leonard/DRK Photo. **A46** (cl) Marilyn Kazmers/Dembinsky Photo Associates. **A46–A47** (bkgd) Avi Klapfer/Mo Yung Productions/Norbert Wu Productions. **A47** (tr) Hans Reinhard/Bruce Coleman, Inc. (cr) © E. R. Degginger/Color Pic, Inc. **A52** (bl) Medford Taylor/National Geographic Image Collection. (bkgd) David Sanger/Alamy Images. **A54** (cr) G. Staebler/Masterfile. (b) Gregory G. Dimijian/Photo Researchers, Inc. **A55** (c) P. Kobeh/Peter Arnold. (bkgd) Tobias Bernhard/Oxford Scientific Library. **A56** © E.R. Degginger/Color Pic, Inc. **A58** (tl) Brian Stablyk/ Photographer's Choice/Getty Images. (tlc) Skip Moody/Dembinsky Photo Associates. (tc) Rod Planck/Photo Researchers, Inc. (tcr) Skip Moody/ Dembinsky Photo Associates. (tr) Marilyn Kazmers/Dembinsky Photo Associates. (bl) Alan & Sandy Carey/Photo Researchers, Inc. (blc) K. McGougan/Bruce Coleman, Inc. (bc) S.Gatzen/EyePress/Photri. (bcr) Dwight Kuhn/Bruce Coleman, Inc. (br) © E.R. Degginger/Color Pic, Inc. **A60–A61** (bkgd) John Cancalosi/Nature Picture Library. **A61** (t) Don & Pat Valenti/DRK Photo. (tc) John Daniels/Ardea. (bc) E.R. Degginger/ Color Pic, Inc. (b) Eric Lindgren/Ardea. **A62** (bl) Nigel Cattlin/Photo Researchers, Inc. **A62–A63** (bkgd) Nigel Cattlin/Photo Researchers, Inc. **A64** John Daniels/Ardea. **A65** Dick Luria/Taxi/Getty Images. **A66** (tl) David R. Frazier/Photo Researchers, Inc. (tr) Don & Pat Valenti/DRK Photo. (cl), (cr) © Dwight Kuhn. **A67** (tl) J.L. Lepore/Photo Researchers, Inc. (tr) Anthony Mercieca/Photo Researchers, Inc. (cl) © Dwight Kuhn. (cr) DK Images. **A68** (tl) The Granger Collection, New York. (b) Academy of Natural Sciences of Philadelphia/Corbis. (frame) Image Farm. **A68–A69** (b) Merian, Maria Sibylla Graff (1647–1717)/Fitzwilliam Museum, University of Cambridge, UK/The Bridgeman Art Library. **A70** (bl) Gary Meszaros/Dembinsky Photo Associates. (br) Bob Jensen/Bruce Coleman, Inc. **A70–71** (bkgd) Michael Hubrich/Dembinsky Photo Associates. **A72** (c) E.R. Degginger/Bruce Coleman, Inc. (b) © E.R. Degginger/Color Pic, Inc. (r) Gary Meszaros/Bruce Coleman, Inc. **A72–A73** (bkgd) Marion Owen/Alaska Stock.com. **A73** (l) E.R. Degginger/Bruce Coleman, Inc. (r) John Shaw/Bruce Coleman, Inc. **A74** (l), (c), (r) © E.R. Degginger/Color Pic, Inc. **A74–A75** (bkgd) Garry Black/Masterfile. **A75** (l), (r) © E.R. Degginger/Color Pic, Inc. A76 (l), (c) © Dwight Kuhn. (r) Gary Meszaros/ Dembinsky Photo Associates. **A78** (tl), (tcl), (tcr), © Dwight Kuhn. (tr) DK Images. **A78** (bl), (bcl), (bcr), (br) © E.R. Degginger/Color Pic, Inc. **A80** (l), (c) Ron Sanford/Corbis. (r) Caudia Adams/Dembinsky Photo Associates. Unit B Opener Rod Williams/Nature Picture Library. **B1** Denver Bryan Photography. **B4–B5** (bkgd) Tim Davis/Corbis. **B5** (t) Jeff Hunter/Getty Images. (tc) John Shaw/Bruce Coleman, Inc. (b) Nigel Cattlin/Photo Researchers, Inc. (bc) Garry Black/Masterfile. **B6** (bl) Fritz Polking/Peter Arnold. **B6–B7** (bkgd) Terry W. Eggers/Corbis. **B8** Tom Soucek/AlaskaStock.com. **B9** (t) Bill Brooks/Masterfile. **B9** (b) Ric Ergenbright/Corbis. **B10** (t) Jeff Hunter/Photographer's Choice/Getty Images. (b) Zigmund Leszczynski/Animals Animals. **B11** (t) David Fritts/ Stone/Getty Images. (cr) Wayne Lynch/DRK Photo. B**12–B13** (bkgd) Darrell Gulin/DRK Photo. **B12** (bl) David T. Roberts/ Nature's Images/ Photo Researchers. **B14–B15** (bkgd) John Shaw/Bruce Coleman, Inc. **B15** (tr) Stephen J. Krasemann/DRK Photo. **B16** (tl) * © Joe McDonald/ Bruce Coleman, Inc. (bl) Gary Meszaros/Bruce Coleman, Inc. (r) Edward Kinsman/Photo Researchers, Inc. **B17** (tl) M.P. Kahl/Photo Researchers, Inc. (tr) Naturfoto Honal/Corbis. (cr) Jim Battles/Dembinsky Photo Associates. B18 (bl) © Gary Meszaros/Dembinsky Photo Associates. **B18–B19** (bkgd) Douglas Faulkner/Corbis. **B20** Colin Varndell/Nature Picture Library. **B21** Jim Zipp/Photo Researchers, Inc. B22 (l) Scott Camazine/Photo Researchers, Inc. (c) Jim Battles/Dembinsky Photo Associates. **B23** (tl) Wayne Bennett/Corbis. (tr) Bill Marchel/Outdoor's Finest Photography. **B24** (bl) Todd Stailey/Courtesy of Tennessee Aquarium. **B24–B25** (bkgd) Tennessee Aquarium. **B26** (bl) Gary Gray/ DRK Photo. **B26–B27** (bkgd) Art Wolfe/ Imagebank/Getty Images. **B28** Nigel Cattlin/ Holt Studio International/Photo Researchers, Inc. **B29** (tr) Breck Kent/Animals Animals. (b) J. E. Swedberg/Bruce Coleman, Inc. **B30** DRK Photo. **B32** (lc) Bill Marchel/Outdoor's Finest Photography. (cr) Zigmund Leszczynski/Animals Animals. (l) Edward Kinsman/Photo Researchers, Inc. (r) David Fritts/ Stone/Getty Images. **B34–B35** (bkgd) Kevin Dodge/Masterfile. **B35** (t) Jean–Michael Cornet/Stock Image/ Pixland/Alamy Images. (b) Richard Hutchings/Photo Edit, Inc. (bc) C Squared Studios/Photodisc/Getty Images. **B36** (bl) Laura Riley/Bruce Coleman, Inc. **B36–B37** (bkgd) Johnny Johnson/DRK Photo.**B38** Harry Rogers/Photo Researchers, Inc. **B39** (l) © Bill Beatty/Wild+Natural. (r) Anup Shah/ Taxi/Getty Images. **B41** (t) Peter Finger/Corbis. (c) Lynn Stone/Index Stock Imagery/PictureQuest. (b) Superstock/PictureQuest. **B46** (br) Brian Sytnyk/Masterfile. **B46–B47** (bkgd) Cosmo Condina/ Getty Images. **B48** (c) J. C. Carton/Bruce Coleman, Inc. (bl) VCL/Taxi/ Getty Images. **B48–B49** (b) David P. Hall/Masterfile. **B49** (tr) Judd Piloss of FoodPix. **B50** Ross Whitaker/Imagebank/Getty Images. **B52** (t) Richard Hutchings/Photo Edit, Inc. (blc) Burke/Triolo/Brand X/ PictureQuest. (bl), (brc) Photodisc/Getty Images. (br) Comstock Images. **B54** (tr) Lynn Stone/Index Stock Imagery/PictureQuest. (bl) Laura Riley/ Bruce Coleman, Inc. (br) Brian Sytnyk/Masterfile. **B56** (l) Mike Kelly/The Image Bank/Getty Images. (c) John Downer/Taxi/Getty Images. (r) Frank Krahmer/The Image Bank/Getty Images. Unit C Opener (bkgd) Index Stock Imagery/Alamy Images. **C1** Gary Ladd Photography. **C4–C5** (bkgd) Arthur M. Greene/Bruce Coleman, Inc. **C5** (t) Tony Freeman/ Photo Edit, Inc. (tc) David Young–Wolff/Photo Edit, Inc. (bc) Rod Planck/ Photo Researchers, Inc. (b) Tom Bean/DRK Photo. **C6–C7** (bkgd) Jeff Foott/Bruce Coleman, Inc. **C8–C9** (bkgd) Dennis MacDonald/Photo Edit Inc. **C9** (tl), (tc) Tony Freeman/Photo Edit Inc. (tr) © Panographics Science Stock. (bl) Roger Wood/Corbis. (bc) Phil Degginger/Color Pic, Inc. (br) Owen Franken/Corbis. **C11** (tl) John William Banagan/ The Image Bank/Getty Images. (tc) E.R. Degginger/Color Pic, Inc. (tr) David Young–Wolff/Photo Edit Inc. **C12** (tl) Hulton Archive/ Stringer/Getty Images. (b) Bettmann/Corbis. **C12–C13** (bkgd) Brian K. Miller/Animals Animals/Earth Scenes. **C13** (t) YardDoctor.com/Briggs and Stratton. (lc) F. Damm/Masterfile. (rc) Jane Grushow/Grant Heilman Photography. **C14–C15** (bkgd) © Susan E. Degginger/Color Pic, Inc. **C16** J. David Andrews/Masterfile. **C17** (tl) E.R. Degginger/Color–Pic, Inc. (tr) Rod Planck/Photo Researchers, Inc. (b) Tom Bean/DRK Photo. **C18** Stephen J. Krasemann/DRK photo. **C19** (t) Brian Miller/Bruce Coleman, Inc. (cr) Thomas Dressler/DRK Photo. **C20** (bl) Francois Gohier/Photo Researchers, Inc. **C20–C21** (bkgd) Kazimieras Mizgiris/AFIAP/Mizgiris Amber Museum. **C23** (tr) Alvis Upitis/Superstock. (cr) William P. Leonard/ DRK Photo. (br) Mindy McNaugher/Stock Photo Archives/Carnegie Museum of Natural History. **C24–C25** (c) DK Images. **C25** (t) Bob Jensen/Bruce Coleman, Inc. (br) Frank Staub/Index Stock Imagery. **C26** (tr) Francois Gohier/Photo Researchers, Inc. (cr) Tom bean/DRK Photo. (br) T. A. WieWandt/DRK Photo. **C27** (br) Bill Aaron/Photo Edit, Inc. **C28** (tr) J. David Andrews/Masterfile. (tl) Rod Planck/Photo Researchers, Inc. (bl) Thomas Dressler/DRK Photo. (br) Brian Miller/Bruce Coleman, Inc. **C30–C31** (bkgd) ©Dwight Kuhn. **C31** (t) Buddy Mays/Corbis. (tc) E.R. Degginger/Color Pic, Inc. (bc) Arnold John Kaplan/Photri. (b) Corbis. **C32** (bl) Jock Montgomery/Bruce Coleman, Inc. **C32–C33** (bkgd) Jonathan Nourok/Photo Edit Inc. **C34** David Young–Wolff/Photo Edit, Inc. **C35** (tl) Susan Van Etten/Photo Edit, Inc. (tr) Ingram Publishing/ Index Stock/Alamy Images. (c) Buddy Mays/Corbis. (br) Michael D. L. Jordan/Dembinsky Photo Associates. (bl) C Squared Studios/Getty Images. **C36** (tl) Michael E. Lubiarz/Dembinsky Photo Associates. **C36–C37** (bkgd) Jeremy Woodhouse/DRK Photo. **C37** (tr) Andrew Rakoczy/ Bruce Coleman, Inc. (cr) ©Phil Degginger/Color Pic, Inc. **C42** (bl) Joe Macdonald/Bruce Coleman, Inc. **C42–C43** (bkgd) E.R. Degginger/Bruce Coleman, Inc. **C44** Paul Conklin/Photo Edit, Inc. **C45** (t) Jonathan Nourok/Photo Edit, Inc. (br) © E.R. Degginger/Color Pic, Inc. **C46** Jim West/The Image Works. **C47** (l) Steven C Kaufman/DRK Photo. **C47** (r) Darrell Gulin/DRK Photo. **C50** Arnold John Kaplan/Photri. **C51** (tl) Superstock. (tr) Charles Orrico/Superstock. (br) Myrleen Ferguson Cate/ Photo Edit, Inc. **C52** Richard Hutchings/Photo Edit, Inc. **C54** (tl) © E.R. Degginger/Color Pic, Inc. (tr) Jim West/The Image Works. (cl) Jonathan Nourok/Photo Edit, Inc. (cr) Steven C Kaufman/DRK Photo. (bl) Emmanuel Faure/SuperStock. (br) Darrell Gulin/DRK Photo. **C56** (l), (c) Courtesy of Spectrum Glass. (r) Kevin Fleming/Corbis. Unit D Opener NTPL/Ian Shaw/The Image Works. **D1** Image Source/PictureQuest. **D4–D5** (bkgd) Warren Faidley/Weather Stock. **D5** (t) Andy Crawford/ DKImages. (tc) Gary Meszaros/Photo Researchers, Inc. (bc) Jeff Foott/ PictureQuest. (b) Jacana/Photo Researchers, Inc. **D6** (bl) Frank LaBua/ Photri. **D6–D7** (bkgd) Corbis. **D8–D9** (bkgd) Don Nauman. **D9** (bc) Tom Warner/Noaa. **D10–D11** (bkgd) Jim Steinberg/Photo Researchers, Inc. **D12** (cl) Gary Meszaros/Photo Researchers, Inc. (b) Scott Smith/Index Stock Imagery. **D13** (t) Jim Mone/AP Wide World Photo. **D14** (bl) Kike Calvo/Bruce Coleman, Inc. **D14–D15** (bkgd) Carol Mallory/Dembinsky Photo Associates. **D15** (inset) Alison Barnes Martin/Masterfile. **D16** (bl) Dawn Charging/Bismark – Mandan CVB. **D17** (cr) Kindra Clineff/Index Stock Imagery. (b) Ralph Krubner/Mira. **D22** (bl) Sid & Shirley Rucker/ DRK Photo. **D22–D23** (bkgd) Maslowski Photo/Photo Researchers, Inc. **D24** (t) Bill Beatty. (b)Fred Habegger/Grant Heilman Photography. **D25** (tl) Harry Rogers/Photo Researchers, Inc. (tc) Thase Daniel/Bruce Coleman Inc. (tr) Edward L. Snow/Bruce Coleman Inc. (bl) Fred Habegger/Grant Heilman Photography. (bc) Geoff Bryant/Photo Researchers, Inc. (br) Fred Habegger/Grant Heilman Photography. **D26** (bl) Photri. (b) Daniel J Cox/Natural Selection Stock Photography. **D27** (tr) Jeff Foott/PictureQuest. (tcr) S. Charles Brown; Frank Lane Picture Agancy/Corbis. (cr) Bill Beatty/Animals Animals. (b) Fred Bruemmer/ DRK Photo. **D30** (tr) Thase Daniel/Bruce Coleman, Inc. (tl) Edward L. Snow/Bruce Coleman Inc. (tcl) Bill Beatty. (tcr) Harry Rogers/Photo Researchers, Inc. (bcl) S. Charles Brown; Frank Lane Picture Agancy/ Corbis. (bcr) Bill Beatty/Animals Animals. (bl) Jeff Foott/PictureQuest. (br) Fred Bruemmer/DRK Photo. **D32–D33** (bkgd) John Henry Williams/ Bruce Coleman, Inc. **D33** (bc) John Sanford/Photo Researchers, Inc. (b) Roger Ressmeyer/Corbis. **D34** (bl) Nasa/Photri. **D34–D35** (bkgd) Nasa/ Photri. **D36** Nasa/Science Photo Library/Photo Researchers, Inc. **D37** (t) © Eric O'Connell/Iconica/Getty Images. **D40** (bl) World Perspectives/ Photographer's Choic/Getty Images. **D40–D41** (bkgd) Bill Aron/Photo Edit, Inc. **D46** (bl) World Perspectives/Stone/Getty Images. **D46–D47** Steven Satushek/Botanica/Getty Images. **D48** World Perspectives/ Stone/Getty Images. **D50–D51** (bkgd) John Sanford/Photo Researchers, Inc. **D54–D55** (bkgd) Bill Frymire/Masterfile. **D56** (cl) Eckhard Slawick/ Photo Researchers, Inc. **D56–D57** (bkgd) Michael Simpson/ Taxi/Getty Images. (cr) Photri. **D57** (cl) Susan McCartney/Photo Researchers, Inc. (br) Photri. **D58** Roger Ressmeyer/Corbis. **D59** (tl) Roger Ressmeyer/ Corbis. (br) John Sanford & David Parker/ Science Photo Library/Photo Researchers, Inc. D64 (l) Owaki–Kulla/Corbis. (r) Tony Arruza/Corbis. Unit E Opener Thinkstock/PictureQuest. **E1** Thinkstock/PictureQuest. **E4–E5** (bkgd) Everett Kennedy Brown, Staff/ European Press Photo Agency, EP/AP Wide World Photo. **E5** (b) Iverson/Folio Inc. **E6** (bl) Gusto/Photo Researchers, Inc. **E6–E7** (bkgd) Thom Lang/Corbis. **E13** (br) G K & Vikki Hart/Getty Images. **E23** (c) Image Courtesy of the United States. **E24** (bl) Skip Moody/Dembinsky Photo Associates, Inc. **E24–E25** (bkgd) George D. Lepp/Corbis. **E26** Ralph A. Clevenger/Corbis. **E27** (t) Jose Luis Pelaez, Inc./Corbis. (lc) Jim Zuckerman/Corbis. (rc) Iverson/ Folio Inc. (b) Greg Wahl–Stephens/AP Wide World Photo. **E28** (tl) Mark A. Schneider/Dembinsky Photo Associates. (tr) Darrell Gulin/Corbis. (tc) Skip Moody/Dembinsky Photo Associates. (bc), (bl) Iverson/Folio Inc. (br) Clouds Hill Imaging Ltd./Corbis. **E32–E33** (bkgd) Daniel Bosler/Stone/ Getty Images. **E33** (b) Gabe Palmer/Corbis. (bc) Premium Stock/Corbis. **E34–E35** (bkgd) Image100/Alamy Images. **E39** Michael Newman/Photo Edit, Inc. **E42** (bl) A. Ramey/Photo Edit, Inc. **E42–E43** David Madison/ Photodisc/Getty Images. **E44** Flip Nicklin/Minden Pictures. **E45** Michael Newman/Photo Edit, Inc. **E46** Michael Newman/PhotoEdit, Inc. **E48–E49** Howie Garber/Animals Animals. **E50** (tl), (br) C. Squared Studios/ Photodisc/Getty Images. (tr), (bl) PhotoDisc/Getty Images. (cl) Premium Stock/Corbis. (cr) Cyril Laubscher/DK Images. **E51** (tl) Gabe Palmer/ Corbis. **E53** (t) C Squared Studios/Getty Images. (l) Photodisc/Getty Images. (r) Steve Cole/Getty Images. (b) David Murray/DK Images. Unit F Opener Tek Image/Photo Researchers Inc. **F1** (bkgd) Steve Taylor/ Stone/Getty Images. **F4–F5** (bkgd) Joe McBride/Photgrapher's Choice/ Getty Images. **F5** (t) Tony Freeman/Photo Edit, Inc. (b) © Phil Degginger/Color–Pic, Inc. **F6–F7** (bkgd) Thinkstock/Getty Images. **F10** (cl) Tony Freeman/Photo Edit, Inc. (br) Picture Plain/Photo Library.com. **F11** (tl) John Fox/Alamy Images. (br) RubberBall Productions/Getty Images. **F12–F13** (bkgd) Rolf Bruderer/Corbis. **F15** (br) Barry Runk/ Grant Heilman Photography. **F16** (tl) Philip Gatward/DK Images. **F17** Rubberball Productions/Getty Images. **F24–F25** David Madison/Stone/ Getty Images. **F25** (tr) Alan Thornton/Stone/Getty Images. **F26** (cr) Bob Daemmrich/Corbis Sygma. **F27** (tr) © E.R. Degginger/Color–Pic Inc. (cr) © Phil Degginger/Color–Pic Inc. F28 (l) Kimberly Robbins/Photo Edit, Inc. **F30** (tc) Barry Runk/Grant Heilman Photography. (tr) Philip Gatward/DK Images. (bl) John Fox/Alamy Images. (bc) Picture Plain/Photo Library. com. (br) Tony Freeman/Photo Edit, Inc. **F33** (tc) Michael Newman/Photo Edit, Inc. **F40** (bl) Michael Newman/Photo Edit, Inc. **F40–F41** (bkgd) Image Source Limited/Index Stock Imagery. **F44** (cr)Tom Pantages. (bl) © E.R. Degginger/Color Pic, Inc. **F45** (tr) © Phil Degginger/Color Pic, Inc. **F46–47** (bkgd) LIU Jin/AFP/Getty Images. **F48** (bl) Tim Pannell/ Corbis. **F56** (r) David Young–Wolf/Photoedit, Inc.

## Assignment

**A6, A7** © HMCo./Ken Karp Photography. **A12, A13, A18** © HMCo./ Richard Hutchings Photography. **A19** © HMCo./Lawrence Migdale Photography. **A24** (tc),(bc) © HMCo./Ken Karp Photography. **A24** (t),(br) © HMCo./Richard Hutchings Photography. **A25** (t) © HMCo./Ken Karp Photography. **A34, A35** © HMCo./Richard Hutchings Photography. **A40, A41, A48, A49, A52, A53, A62, A63** © HMCo./Ken Karp Photography. **A70** (bc) © HMCo./Richard Hutchings Photography **A70** (t),(tc),(b) **A71** © HMCo./Ken Karp Photography. **B6** (t) © HMCo./Richard Hutchings Photography. **B7** © HMCo./Lawrence Migdale Photography. **B12, B13, B18, B26, B27, B36, B37, B46, B47** © HMCo./Richard Hutchings Photography. **C6, C7, C14, C15, C20, C21, C32, C33** © HMCo./Richard Hutchings Photography. **C38** © HMCo./Ken Karp Photography. **C42, C43, C48, C49** © HMCo./Richard Hutchings Photography. **D6, D7** © HMCo./Richard Hutchings Photography. **D14** (c) © HMCo./Ken Karp Photography. **D14** (t) © HMCo./Richard Hutchings Photography. **D15,D20** © HMCo./Ken Karp Photography. **D22, D23, D28, D34, D35, D40, D41** © HMCo./Richard Hutchings Photography. **D43** © HMCo./Bud Endress Photography. **D46, D47, D54** (t), (bc), (b) © HMCo./Coppola Studios Inc. **D54** (bl) © HMCo./Ken Karp Photography. **D55** © HMCo./Richard Hutchings Photography. **E5** © HMCo./Ken Karp Photography. **E6** (t), (tc), (bc) © HMCo./Richard Hutchings Photography. **E6** (b) © HMCo./Ken Karp Photography. **E7** © HMCo./Richard Hutchings Photography. **E10–E11** © HMCo./Bud Endress Photography. **E12** © HMCo./Richard Hutchings Photography. **E13** © HMCo./Ken Karp Photography. **E14, E15** © HMCo./Richard Hutchings Photography. **E16, E17, E18, E19, E20, E21** © HMCo./Ken Karp Photography. **E24, E25, E33** (t) © HMCo./Richard Hutchings Photography. **E33** (tc), **E34** (bl) © HMCo./Ken Karp Photography. **E34** (t), (tc), (bc), (b), **E35, E36–E37, E38, E42, E43, E48, E49, E51, E52** © HMCo./Richard Hutchings Photography. **F5** (tc) © HMCo./Lawrence Migdale Photography. **F5** (bc), **F6** (b) © HMCo./Ken Karp Photography. **F6** (tr), **F7** © HMCo./Richard Hutchings Photography. **F8–F9** © HMCo./ Ken Karp Photography. **F12, F13** HMCo./Richard Hutchings Photography. **F14** © HMCo./Ken Karp Photography. **F15, F16** © HMCo./ Lawrence Migdale Photography. **F18, F20** © HMCo./Ken Karp Photography. **F22** © HMCo./Richard Hutchings Photography. **F22** (bkgd) © HMCo./Ken Karp Photography. **F23** © HMCo./Richard Hutchings Photography. **F26** © HMCo./Ken Karp Photography. **F30** © HMCo./Ken Karp Photography. **F33** (t) © HMCo./Richard Hutchings Photography. **F33** (bc) © HMCo./Ken Karp Photography. **F34, F35, F36, F37** © HMCo./Richard Hutchings Photography. **F38** © HMCo./Ken Karp Photography. **F39, F40, F41,** © HMCo./Richard Hutchings Photography. **F42, F43, F48** (bl) © HMCo./Ken Karp Photography. **F48** (t), **F49** © HMCo./Richard Hutchings Photography. **F51, F52** © HMCo./Ken Karp Photography.

## Illustration

**A5** Wendy Smith. **A8** Jeff Wack. **A15, A26–A27** Wendy Smith. **A28** Lori Anzalone. **A48–A51** Liz Conrad. **B16–B17** Luigi Galante. **B20–B21** Michael Maydak. **B22–B23** Patrick Gnan. **B35** © Lelend Klanderman. **B40–B4**3 © Leland Klanderman. **B51** Argosy Publishing. **B54** © Leland Klanderman. **C10** Richard Orr. **C22–C23** Michigan Science Art. **C26** Michael Maydak. **C38–C41** Theresa Smythe. **C48** Tim Johnson. **C50–C51** Digital Dimensions. **D16–D17** Robert Schuster. **D16–17** (map) Annette Cable. **D18–D19** Kristin Barr. **D21** Mark & Rosemary Jarman. **D20–D21** (bkgd) JoAnn Adinolfi. **D33** (t) Bob Kayganich. **D33** (tc) Patrick Gnan. **D38–D39** Bob Kayganich. **D42** Patrick Gnan. **D44** Argosy. **D49** Patrick Gnan. **D59** Matthew Trueman. **D60** Argosy Publishing. **E14–E15, E18–E19** Tim Johnson. **E22–E23** Robert Schuster. **E30** Terri Chicko **E33, E38** Sharon and Joel Harris. **E40** Laura Ovresat. **E41** Shane McGowan. **E47** Patrick Gnan. **E54** Terri Chicko. **E56** David Klug. **F18–F21** John Berg. **F28** George Baquero. **F47, F56** Patrick Gnan.

## Nature of Science

PHOTOGRAPHY: (solar disc) © Brand X Pictures/The Stocktrek Corp/ Alamy Images. **S1** © Jose Luis Pelaez, Inc./CORBIS. **S2-3** JSC/NASA. **S4-5** © Ernest Manewal/Superstock. **S5** (br) © HMCo./Ed Imaging. **S6-7** Stephen Dalton/NHPA. **S7** (r) © HMCo./Ed Imaging. **S8-9** © HMCo./Joel Benjamin Photography. **S10-1** Lloyd C. French/JPL/NASA. **S11** (r) © Reuters/CORBIS. **S12-3** (bkgd) © David Martyn Hughes/Alamy Images. **S12-3** (l) (m) (r) © HMCo./Bruton Stroube. **S14-15** © Craig Steven Thrasher/Alamy Images. **S16** © HMCo./Richard Hutchings Photography.

## Health and Fitness Handbook

PHOTOGRAPHY: **H10** © Ariel Skelley/Corbis. **H13** George Shelley/ Masterfile. **H14** (t) Picturequest. (b) Photodisc/Getty Images. **H15** (t) Brad Rickerby/Getty Images. (m) Rubberball/Getty Images. (b) Photodisc/Getty Images. **H16** (t) Dex Image/Getty Images. (b) Ariel Skelley/Corbis.
ILLUSTRATION: **H18–H19** William Melvin. **H23** Linda Lee.

## Science and Math Toolbox

**H7** (t) John Giustina/Getty Images. (m) Georgette Douwma/Getty Images. (b) Giel/Getty Images. **H8** Photodisc/Getty Images.

H40 • Credits